THE INCAS

TIM WOOD

Heinemann

Acknowledgements

The publishers would like to thank Bill Le Fever, who illustrated the see-through pages; James Field, who illustrated the cover; and the organizations that have given their permission to reproduce the following pictures:

American Museum of Natural History/Courtesy Department Library Services Tr.5004(2) /Photo by John Bigelow Taylor: 44 above right.
Ancient Art and Architecture Collection: 29 below right, 30 above left, 34 above left, 35 above right.
Bildarchiv Preussischer Kulturbesitz/Staatliche Museen zu Berlin - Museum für Volkekunde: 12 below left.
Bridgeman Art Library/British Museum, London: 44 below right, /Gilray 45 above right.
The Art Institute of Chicago. Photograph copyright 1994. All Rights Reserved. South America, North Coast Peru, Lambeyeque Valley, Chimu-Inca style, Ritual vessel representing woman with an aryballos, ceramic c.1480, 23.8 x 18.4 cm Buckingham Fund 1955.2411. Photograph by Robert Hashimoto: 31 above right.
E.T. Archive/National Museum Archaeology, Lima: 27 above right.
Werner Forman Archive/Museum für Volkekunde, Berlin: 12 above left, 17 above right, 26 below left, 26 above right, 29 above centre, 45 below left.
Photographie Giraudon: 18 above left, 19 above right.
Robert Harding Picture Library: 15 above right, /Amano Museum, Lima 26 above left, /Robert Frerck 28 above left, /Christopher Rennie 18 above right.
Michael Holford: 4 above left, 5 below right, 7 below right.
Magnum Photos/Stuart Franklin: 9 above right, 36 above centre left, 36 above left.
MAS: 42 above left. **South American Pictures:** 6 above left, 23 below right, 37 below right, 43 above right, /Tony Morrison 11 above right, 21 below right, 29 above right, 35 below right.
The Textile Museum, Washington, D.C./91.395: 29 above left.

Illustrators:
Peter Bull: 5, 14 top left. **James Field (Simon Girling):** cover. **Ray Grinaway:** title page, 4, 8, 9 bottom right, 10, 10-11, 20, 21, 28.
Christian Hook: 14, 15, 18, 19, 26-27. **Richard Hook (Linden Artists):** 46-47. **Bill Le Fever:** 16-17, 24-25, 32-33, 40-41.
Tony Randall: 22, 23 (both), 30, 31, 44. **Mark Stacey:** 6-7, 7, 9 top right, 12, 13, 38-39, 39, 42, 43. **Simon Williams:** 34, 35, 36-37, 37.

Editor: Andrew Farrow
Designers: Mark Summersby and Nick Avery
Picture researcher: Anna Smith
Production controllers: Christine Campbell and David Lawrence

Other titles in the series:
The Aztecs, Ancient Rome, Ancient Greece, Ancient Egypt, The Middle Ages, The Renaissance, The Vikings, The Age of Industry, Forts & Castles, Tombs & Treasure, The Celts, Plains Indians, Houses & Homes, Submarines & Ships, The Apaches and Pueblo Peoples of the Southwest.

First published in Great Britain 1996
by Heinemann Children's Reference,
an imprint of Heinemann Publishers (Oxford) Ltd,
Halley Court, Jordan Hill, Oxford, OX2 8EJ.

MADRID ATHENS PARIS
FLORENCE PRAGUE WARSAW
PORTSMOUTH NH CHICAGO SAO PAULO
SINGAPORE TOKYO MELBOURNE AUCKLAND
IBADAN GABORONE JOHANNESBURG

ISBN 0 600 58683 9

A CIP catalogue record for this book is available at the British Library.

Books printed and bound by Proost, Belgium.

CONTENTS

ORIGINS OF THE INCAS

The Incas learned goldworking skills from peoples they conquered, like the Chimus. This 12th-13th century Chimu vase is made of gold and decorated with turquoises.

About **50,000** years ago, the first people came to North America across a land bridge which joined north-east Asia to Alaska. By about **10,000** BC their descendants had moved into South America. Some became hunter-gatherers in the lush Amazonian rainforest. Others became farmers in what is now Peru. It was from this group, about **6,000** years ago, that the first significant South American civilizations emerged.

A HARD LAND

The western side of South America is a harsh, mountainous region dominated by the craggy peaks of the Andes mountains. South America contains almost every type of climate and landscape from lifeless deserts to lush jungles. Annual average temperatures vary from over 27°C (80°F) in the tropical north to below zero in the south. In the east of the region lie some of the wettest places on Earth with an amazing annual rainfall of 10 metres. In contrast, the Atacama Desert in the west is probably the driest region in the world, with an average annual rainfall of zero. The terrain, which contains glaciers, salt pans, mineral-fouled lakes and some of the world's most active volcanoes, is often shaken by major earthquakes.

THE FIRST CIVILIZATIONS

Peru is a very mountainous country that has very little level farming land. The desolate high plains, called *punas*, are too cold to cultivate. The barren coastal plain is mainly desert. The best areas for cultivation and living are the river valleys. About 10,000 years ago, many small communities sprang up along the banks of the rivers which emptied into the Pacific. But there were only six main regions able to support large groups of people.

DEVELOPING SKILLS

At first the people lived in stone or mud-brick huts. They ate fish, potatoes and beans. But as each culture learned from and adopted the ideas of earlier cultures, new skills developed. The first large civilization, the Chavin culture, flourished in the northern highlands of the Andes from 850 to 350 BC. The Chavins built terraces for growing crops, grain stores to preserve their harvests, and temples where they worshipped a cat god. Their craftsmen produced many beautiful gold and silver objects.

Chimu goldsmiths at work. They blew through long metal tubes to make the charcoal fire burn hotter. Although the Andean peoples made many wonderful objects in gold, most of them have disappeared - melted down by the Spanish conquistadors.

CRAFTWORK DEVELOPS

The Mochicas, a northern coastal group, were at the height of their power about AD 800. Their craftworkers made fine pottery, metalwork and cloth. They built roads and organized a messenger system. The Paracas, to the south, wove elaborate textiles and made unusual terracotta figurines. They also mummified their dead. Further south, the Nazca civilization designed beautiful textiles and constructed elaborate graves, one of which contained over 500 bodies.

CITY BUILDERS

The Empire of Tiahuanaco grew on the shores of Lake Titicaca from about AD 900 to 1300. The Tiahuanacoans were skilled stone-workers. They built a great religious centre with huge pyramids, giant statues, enormous courtyards and terraces. The moon-worshipping Chimus, whose kingdom lasted from about AD 1150 to 1450, perfected the art of city-building. The largest of their mud brick cities, Chanchan, which had a population of 100,000, was probably the most symmetrical city ever built. The Chimus mass-produced pottery (mostly black), made superb feather tunics and did large-scale gold working. But by 1450, all the earlier empires had disappeared. They had been conquered and absorbed by the greatest Andean tribe, the Incas.

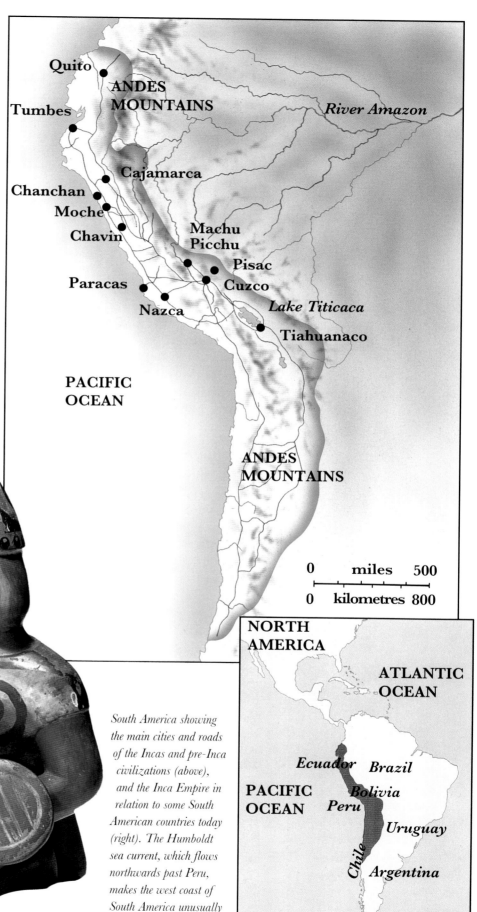

A 6th or 7th century Mochica clay statuette showing a warrior carrying a club and shield. He wears a helmet over a cloth hood which hides the large plugs he wears in his ears. Inca warriors looked similar to this.

South America showing the main cities and roads of the Incas and pre-Inca civilizations (above), and the Inca Empire in relation to some South American countries today (right). The Humboldt sea current, which flows northwards past Peru, makes the west coast of South America unusually cold and dry.

THE EMPIRE

No obstacle was too great for the Incas to overcome and there must have been many spectacular cliff-top attacks (right). The Incas had no technological advantage over their enemies, but the Incas had a superior supply system and they usually outnumbered their foes.

In AD 1300 the Incas were a small and insignificant tribe. During the next 200 years they expanded at a fantastic rate. By 1500, they controlled an empire which rivalled that of ancient Rome. It contained over 12 million people and stretched a distance of 4,000 kilometres down the west coast of South America.

THE FIRST INCAS

The Incas called themselves the *Quechua* tribe. The word Inca means 'lord' in *Quechua*, the Incas' language, and they used it only to describe their rulers. We now use the word Inca to describe all the people who were ruled by this civilization. The Incas didn't invent a writing system, so little is known about their early history which consists mainly of half-remembered legends. It is likely that the tribe settled in a valley high in the Andes where they built their capital, Cuzco, in about 1300. At that time there was little to distinguish the Incas from their warlike neighbours. It was not until after 1438, when Inca Pachacuti became their ruler, that the Incas began to expand their territory at an amazing rate.

THE ALL-CONQUERING INCAS

Pachacuti seems to have been a military genius. He led spectacular campaigns that massively increased the land area of the developing Inca empire. The rugged Andean landscape, while creating many difficulties for the advancing Incas, also helped them. The tribes who opposed the Incas were scattered over small areas of fertile land in isolated, steep-sided valleys. These tribes could not join together to resist the Incas who were able to conquer them one by one. With each new conquest the Inca army grew. As they advanced, the Incas built roads and fortresses to guard their new conquests, and storehouses to hold supplies for the army. In this way they were able to keep an iron grip over the areas they conquered.

TOPA YUPANQUI

After about 10 years of war, Pachacuti gave his son Topa Yupanqui the task of pursuing the Incas' conquests while he concentrated on ruling his people and rebuilding Cuzco. Topa conquered the highlands and the coastal plains. He even invaded the Amazon rainforest, but it was here that the Incas met their first defeats. They were unable to penetrate the thick jungle. They also met fierce resistance from the Araucanian tribe far to the south. The two sides fought one of the bloodiest battles of medieval times which lasted for three days and left thousands dead and wounded. Eventually the Incas withdrew, accepting this as the most southerly point of their empire.

THE GROWING EMPIRE

As the campaigns continued, tribes which did not accept Inca rule were conquered. Those which did accept Inca rule were absorbed peacefully into the empire. The Incas demanded that their new subjects follow the Inca way of life. They provided teachers to show the conquered tribes how to build villages, storehouses and irrigation ditches to improve their agriculture. Enormous quantities of booty flowed back to Cuzco.

GOVERNMENT

While the empire grew, Pachacuti was laying down the foundations of Inca rule. He devised a code of laws which extended Inca control throughout the empire. He standardized the calendar into 12 months of 30 days. He made Sun worship the official state religion and replaced all non-Inca festivals with new ceremonies for worshipping the Sun. He made himself, as emperor, not only the most powerful person in Peru, but also one of its most important gods. He made Cuzco the spectacular capital of the empire.

The tribespeople of this village have been conquered by the Incas. Peasants are taken as slaves, while the sons of the conquered chief are sent to Cuzco to be trained in the Inca way of ruling. Tribes which could not accept the Inca way of life were simply settled somewhere else. Their lands were given to tribes whose loyalty was beyond doubt.

Booty taken from the conquered tribes was sent back to Cuzco. This gold vessel in the shape of a dove was probably used for ceremonial purposes by the Chimu tribe that made it.

THE INCA PEOPLE

The people who lived in the Inca empire were members of different tribes which had either been conquered by the Incas, or had accepted Inca rule. Most of them were poor peasant farmers, struggling to wring out a living from the harsh and unforgiving landscape. Under Inca rule they became one of the most organized and regimented societies that has ever existed.

Each autumn the land was divided among the members of the ayllu. *Here a newly married couple are leaving a meeting hall after being allocated a piece of land to farm.*

FAMILY GROUPS

From the earliest times the Andean people realized that they needed to work together in order to survive. Many tribes were organized into extended family groups or clans called *ayllus* which were ruled by elected leaders and guided by councils of old men. The Incas adopted the *ayllu* and used them as the basis for organizing their empire. Everyone was born into an *ayllu* and remained a lifelong member. Each *ayllu* looked after its own members. Some *ayllus* were small; others could be very large. For example, the inhabitants of a large city such as Cuzco were, in effect, members of the same *ayllu*.

THE DIVISION OF THE LAND

Under Inca rule, each *ayllu* had its own territory and was responsible for farming the land within it. Every autumn, the land was divided among the *ayllu's* members, all of whom were loaned as much as they needed to support their families for the coming year. In practice this meant that each married couple had a piece of land roughly 100 metres by 50 metres. Larger families were given extra land to farm.

TRIBUTE

Each family was responsible for its own piece of land. Some land was set aside for the Sapa Inca (the emperor), and some for the Sun God. The peasants worked the Sapa Inca's land and the Sun God's land as a kind of labour tax. About one-third of all the crops and animals produced by an *ayllu* went as tribute to the Sapa Inca, one-third went to the Sun temples, and about one-third was kept by the *ayllu*.

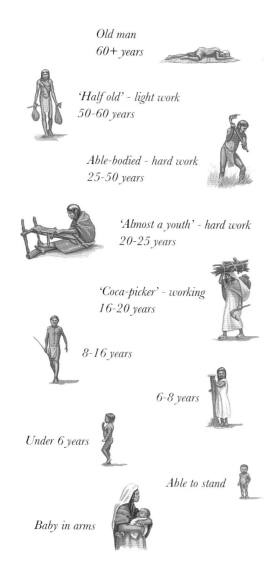

Old man
60+ years

'Half old' - light work
50-60 years

Able-bodied - hard work
25-50 years

'Almost a youth' - hard work
20-25 years

'Coca-picker' - working
16-20 years

8-16 years

6-8 years

Under 6 years

Able to stand

Baby in arms

The divisions of the ayllu. *The main work was done by those aged 16 to 60. The rest were still expected to do whatever work they could manage, however young or old they were.*

DIVISION OF THE PEOPLE

Each *ayllu* was subdivided into groups of 'tax-payers'. These were the able-bodied people who could pay the labour tax by working on the land and doing craft work. They also had to pay the *mit'a* (public duty tax) by serving in the army and working on state projects. The groups were based on units of 10 - the smallest contained 10 people, the largest contained 10,000. In order to distinguish which people were able to pay their taxes, the whole of the population was also grouped according to age. There were 10 categories of men and 10 of women. Each group was expected to contribute as much as it could to the life of the community unless the members were too young or too old to be useful.

ADULTHOOD

Once they were 25, men passed into the category of *hatun-runa* or *puric*, meaning able-bodied. They were eligible to pay both the labour tax and the *mit'a*. Women reached adulthood earlier than men. They looked after their menfolk as well as weaving cloth and helping on the land. Above the age of 60, men were expected to perform only the lightest of duties. Women were expected to look after the children. Once past 80, men and women were thought to be old, hard of hearing, and able only to eat and sleep. They were looked after by other members of the *ayllu* and could draw what food and clothing they needed from state storehouses, or *qollas* (see page 36).

Old people, such as the old woman below, could draw food and clothing they needed from the state storehouses. The official is recording her share using a quipu *(see page 12). In the background, workers are serving their* mit'a.

An original Inca helmet made of woven straw covered with llama wool and cotton. The black square may have been a clan 'totem' or symbol. Each Inca tribe had its own totem.

THE SAPA INCA

The ruler of the Incas was the Sapa Inca. He was not just the emperor. He was thought to be a direct descendant of the Sun and, as such, he was a god. All the land, people and wealth of the Incas belonged to him. His every command had to be obeyed without question.

THE SUN GOD

His people thought of the Sapa Inca as the Sun God who could be pitiless to his enemies but was always kind to his people. The Sapa Inca was surrounded by amazing wealth and elaborate ceremony at all times. He ate and drank from golden plates and goblets held by his personal servants, the Chosen Women (see pages 22 and 23). Although the Sapa Inca wore clothes similar in style to his subjects, they were much finer. Each day he put on new clothes which had been specially made for him by Chosen Women using only the best quality alpaca and vicuña wool. Each day his uneaten food and the clothes from the previous day were laid aside to be ceremonially burned.

GOLDEN THRONE

The Sapa Inca sat on a golden throne. A Spanish chronicler described how visitors to the Sapa Inca's court had to wear burdens strapped to their backs to show him respect. When the Sapa Inca spat, a female servant caught the spittle in her hand. If one of his hairs fell on his clothing, a female servant removed and ate it.

Mummies played an important part in Inca festivals. Most mummies were dried naturally in the dry, cold air of the mountains, without using artificial preservatives. Here some mummies are being paraded during the Festival of the Dead. The mummies were sat in a row, in order of seniority, and waited on by servants.

The Sapa Inca on his throne with various symbols of his authority including a royal headdress made of wool. The Sapa Inca sometimes carried a small standard made of stiffened cloth which may have been a kind of sceptre.

OFFICIAL HISTORY

When the Sapa Inca died, the whole of the empire went into mourning. A council decided what memories of his life should be preserved. These were then recorded on *quipus* (see pages 12 and 13) and became the official history. Rememberers were instructed what to say about the dead lord. The destruction of *quipus* by Spanish priests, who thought they were the books of the devil, as well as the dying out of rememberers, resulted in much Inca history being lost.

ROYAL MUMMIES

The body of the dead Sapa Inca was preserved through a process known as mummification. His personal servants were ceremonially strangled so they could serve their ruler in the afterlife.

But the old ruler was not thought of as dead. The royal mummies were regarded as visible links between the people and the gods, and were kept in great luxury as symbols of life after death. All the palaces, lands, servants and belongings of a Sapa Inca remained his property after his death. His house in Cuzco became a shrine. All of the Sapa Inca's male descendants, except for the one chosen as his successor, became the courtiers of the dead Inca.

THE WEALTH OF THE MUMMIES

Each Sapa Inca's mummy was served with food as if it was still alive. It played an important part in many religious ceremonies. Mummies were even taken to visit each other!

'The dead toasted one another, and they drank to the living and vice versa; this was done by their ministers in their names...'

— *Bernabé Cobo* —

This system had a great effect on the position of a new Sapa Inca. He inherited tremendous power but no land, because the mummy of the previous ruler kept all the royal property. The Sapa Inca's wealth came from the labour his subjects did for him - farming his land, fighting for the army or working on public projects. In order to feed the workers and to increase the number of people paying the labour tax, the Sapa Inca needed more land. Without land, an Inca ruler could not govern and, even more important, his cult would not last after his death. This system might help to explain the rapid expansion of the Inca empire, as each new Sapa Inca conquered land for himself.

This golden mask is shaped to represent the Sun God. In theory, all gold in the empire belonged to the Sapa Inca.

A quipu *was a bundle of knotted cords used by the Incas to keep records. The secret of how* quipus *worked has been lost but it seems likely that the position, colour and length of the cords, as well as the number and size of the knots, were all significant.*

This group of pottery figures shows a drunken Inca being helped home by his neighbours. People often got drunk during festivals by drinking ceremonial maize beer called chicha. *Drunkenness was not considered a crime in Inca society.*

The Inca emperors ruled an enormous empire, which they called *Tahuantinsuyu*, or the Land of the Four Quarters. They did this without a writing system or knowledge of the wheel or iron. In spite of these disadvantages, the government was highly organized and Inca laws rigidly enforced. Incas received merciless punishments for committing crimes.

PACHACUTI'S LAWS

The Incas' laws were like a collection of traditions and customs with everyone knowing what was taboo (forbidden for religious reasons) and what the penalties were for breaking a taboo. In about 1450 Pachacuti simplified and reorganized these traditions and customs. His laws were administered by the officials who had been appointed to control each group of people.

THE PYRAMID STATE

Inca society was organized rather like a pyramid. People at each level of the pyramid obeyed orders from those immediately above them. At the top was the Sapa Inca. All commands came from him. He was emperor, chief priest, commander-in-chief and son of the Sun God.

Under the Sapa Inca were the nobles, who were mostly his relatives. They were appointed as councillors to advise the Sapa Inca, and as governors of the provinces. The most important officials administered the Sapa Inca's far-flung lands, acting as the eyes and ears of the emperor.

In court each party told their side of the story to a curaca *who then passed judgement. Sentences could be reduced for murderers who killed in self-defence or because they lost control through anger.*

In order to rule efficiently, the Sapa Inca had to know what was happening inside his empire. One of the ways this was achieved was by carrying out regular censuses. The results were recorded on quipus. *In this way the Sapa Inca knew all the resources of the empire. The censuses were carried out by the emperor's envoy, called a* runaquipa.

HARSH PUNISHMENTS

Punishments were very harsh as crimes against the state were also crimes against the Sapa Inca and thus against the Sun God. There was no system of imprisonment. The first occurrence of a minor crime might meet with a public telling-off. Second offences might lead to death by hanging, stoning, or by pushing the offender over a cliff. The death penalty was given for murder, stealing, breaking into state storage chambers, damaging bridges or entering the rooms of Chosen Women. Laziness, which was considered a very serious crime, as lazy people were depriving the Sapa Inca of their work, was also punishable by death. The upper classes were punished more severely than the peasants, because higher standards were expected from them. Public rebuke for the common people became banishment for the nobility. Where ordinary taxpayers were tortured or mutilated, nobles would be put to death.

THE CURACAS

Beneath the nobles was a class of less important nobles called *curacas*. These were people who held important administrative posts in the empire, but were not full-blooded Incas. The Inca Empire had expanded so rapidly that there were not enough pure Incas to rule it. When a new territory was overrun, the Incas allowed the chiefs of the conquered tribes to continue governing. The sons of the chiefs were taken away to Cuzco to be taught how to rule in the Inca way. Inca nobles and *curacas* did not pay any taxes.

Beneath the *curacas* were lesser officials known as the *caramayoc* (village headmen). They were responsible for enforcing the law at a local level. Each headman was responsible for a certain number of peasant households.

Pushing a criminal off a cliff was a simple and effective form of execution which had been used by Indian tribes in the Andes for hundreds, if not thousands, of years.

CUZCO – THE CAPITAL CITY

A plan of Cuzco, showing its shape like a crouching puma. The city, which housed about 100,000 people, was cleaner and better maintained than most European cities of the time. The festival held to celebrate the city's founding took place in spring. First, the city was 'cleansed' of evil spirits. Relays of royal princes carrying spears chased the spirits out of the city along the four main roads (below). Outside the city, the lances were driven into the ground. These formed a barrier which would keep evil spirits away for another year.

The city of Cuzco lay in a mountain valley about 4,000 metres above sea level. Cuzco, which means 'navel' in the *Quechua* language, was rebuilt by Pachacuti and made the centre of his empire.

PACHACUTI'S DESIGN

Pachacuti restored the palaces of former emperors and built a magnificent one for himself, called the *Cassana*. He designed and built the *Accla Huasi*, the house of the 4,000 Chosen Women of the Sun God. He laid out gardens filled with trees, flowers and herbs. Each year a festival was held to celebrate the founding of the city. The festival coincided with celebrations of the arrival of spring. First, the Sapa Inca hailed the Sun God. Next, royal princes chased evil spirits out of the city. Later, ritual bathing got rid of any remaining evil, and then everyone danced and sang all night. Finally everyone rubbed their bodies and houses with *sanko* (maize paste) to ward off illness and weakness.

REFLECTION OF THE EMPIRE

The city was divided into four quarters which echoed the division of the empire; so, for example, people from the eastern part of the empire lived in the eastern part of the city. The *curacas* built their homes in the correct quarter surrounded by their subjects. Walking through the city was like walking through the empire.

THE CITY OF THE PUMA

The inner city of Cuzco was laid out in the shape of a puma. The head was the fortress of Sacsahuamán (which means 'imperial falcon') in the north of the city, and the tail was a public garden in the south. The heart was the *Huacapata*, or holy square, containing the Coricancha or Temple of the Sun. Within the puma was a grid of narrow, paved streets, each with a stone channel carrying fresh mountain water. These helped citizens keep their homes clean and healthy. In addition, people regularly bathed in the Huatanay and the Tullumayo rivers, which flowed along either flank of the puma. Only members of the royal *ayllu* and the most important citizens lived in the inner city. Ordinary citizens lived in the suburbs outside the puma.

SACSAHUAMÁN

The city was guarded by the fortress of Sacsahuamán. This was built into the steep-sided hill which overlooked Cuzco. The south face of the hill was a sheer cliff. The other sides of the city were guarded by gigantic terraced walls which rose one above the other. Sacsahuamán contained an arsenal, a temple, a huge parade-ground, palaces, vaults, reservoirs, store rooms and the throne of the Inca. The Spaniards were awestruck by the fortress.

'Many who have visited it, and who have travelled in Lombardy and other foreign countries, say they have never seen a building to compare with it. Nothing built by the Romans is as impressive as this.'

Sancho

The fortress of Sacsahuamán stood on a hill above Cuzco. The remains of part of the enormous zig-zag walls with their doorways can be seen in this view.

OBSERVATORIES

The Incas also built simple astronomical observatories. Priests used these to observe the Sun and planets. This helped them calculate the passing of the seasons so that the farming cycle of ploughing, planting and harvesting could proceed at the right times. Many observatories consisted of a single pillar placed to allow priests to measure the progress of the Sun through the sky. Others were more elaborate.

An Inca observatory. The Spaniards described how the observatories in Cuzco consisted of eight stone pillars on the eastern side of the city and eight on the western side. These were organized into two rows of four and stood about seven metres apart on specially raised and levelled ground. On the tops of the pillars were discs through which the Sun's rays could pass. Lines drawn on the ground marked the passage of the Sun across the sky.

15

PALACE ON THE LAKE

The see-through scene below shows the Palace of the Inca and the Convent of the Chosen Women on islands on Lake Titicaca. The reconstructions are based on a few remains on the islands and descriptions of Spanish chroniclers and later travellers. In fact, the islands were several kilometres apart. On the lake, a procession of reed boats sails by. In the distance are the floating homes of Uru tribespeople, built on islands made of reeds.

While Cuzco was the centre of government, Lake Titicaca was the legendary birthplace of the first Incas. One Inca myth tells of a great flood after which the first rays of the Sun fell on one of the islands. Here the Sun created his children, the Incas.

LAKE OF THE JAGUAR

Lake Titicaca is the highest navigable lake in the world. At 3,812 metres above sea level, those unused to the height gasp for breath at the slightest effort. No one is sure what Titicaca means. Some people have said it means Wild Cat Lake or, perhaps, Lake of the Jaguar. The lake is about 200 km long and contains 25 islands. On the lake's shores lived the Uru tribe which had been absorbed into the Inca Empire.

ISLAND OF THE SUN

The most important part of the lake was an island which the Incas called the Island of the Sun. The island contained a single temple called the Palace of the Inca. This was a two-storey building, about 16 metres by 14 metres. But although it was small, the temple was fabulously wealthy. It stands at the point which legend claims was the birthplace of the first Incas. It is probable that the Sapa Inca made an annual pilgrimage there.

At one end of Lake Titicaca there was a bridge that crossed a river flowing into the lake. This drawing is based on a sketch made by a Spanish chronicler.

SACRED CORN

The rest of the island was transformed by terracing into a vast garden. Here priests grew sacred maize seeds. The harvest from these was considered to be a symbol of the fertility of the whole of the Inca lands. The corn grown on the island was distributed every year to all the temples of the empire.

THE ISLAND OF THE MOON

Many Andean people, particularly those who lived in the hot, lower regions and feared the fierce heat of the sun, worshipped the moon instead. Both Sun and Moon worship seem to have been practised at Lake Titicaca. The moon was probably worshipped at Coati, the Island of the Moon, which was next to the Island of the Sun. This contained a much larger building which is known as the Temple of the Moon. However, it was almost certainly an *acclahausi* (home) for Chosen Women serving the Moon God. Unusually for an Inca building, the walls were coated with mud plaster. Shapes and decorations were pressed into the mud and the whole building was painted yellow and red.

Maize was thought to be sacred by the Incas and was cultivated on the Island of the Sun. The Spanish conquerors were astounded to discover that the gardens around Coricancha in Cuzco were planted with lifesize maize plants made of gold and silver, similar to the one shown here.

1 **Island of the Moon**
2 **Temple of the Chosen Women**
3 **Stepped niches**
4 **Island of the Sun**
5 **Palace of the Inca**
6 **Corbelled vaults**
7 **Reed boats**
8 **Uru floating islands**

ENGINEERING THE LAND

A partially restored building. Notice the clean rockface at the top where stone was split away. The face may have been smoothed with sand. The walls below have been repaired with modern cement, but the shapes of the stones can be clearly seen.

Inca stoneworkers split blocks of stone from the rockface with wooden wedges. These were shaped with stone or obsidian tools and moved around by brute force. Great public works such as temples took years to build.

The Incas were very skilful engineers who learned how to shape the land to suit their needs. Using only the simplest tools and massive human effort, they created public works which still amaze engineers today.

TERRACING

Much of the land in the Inca Empire was hard to farm. Where there was sufficient rainfall, the ground sloped too steeply for farming, and the rain washed away the soil. Where the land was flat enough to work, there was too little rainfall. So the Incas increased the amount of farming land in two main ways. The first, and most spectacular, was by terracing the hillsides. The second was by digging canals to irrigate (water) the land.

All major engineering projects were planned by professional architects sent from Cuzco. All the work was done by hand. Elaborate terracing schemes transformed steep hillsides into great flights of stone steps which supported flat fields. These greatly increased the amount of land which could be farmed, and also stopped the rain washing away the soil.

A typical piece of Inca stonework. The perfect joints between each differently shaped stone took many hours to shape.

IRRIGATION

In areas where rain was scarce, engineers built reservoirs and cisterns to store water. Many of these were underground and lined with stone to prevent the water evaporating. An elaborate network of canals and ditches was constructed. These carried water from wetter areas and from mountain streams to irrigate the fields and fill the cisterns. The engineers also dammed and straightened rivers to improve the flow and reduce erosion of the fertile banks.

SCIENTIFIC KNOWLEDGE

These works showed that the Incas had a good knowledge of practical science. Inca engineers were able to introduce water on the top step of a terrace and direct it to run down, watering each of the steps below in turn. They knew how water which flowed too fast could erode the banks of a stream and that water which flowed too slowly would allow weeds to grow which in turn could block a channel.

To make the land more productive, they used the huge deposits of guano (bird droppings) found along the coast as fertilizer. They considered this resource so important that killing seabirds became a crime punishable by death!

BUILDING

Nowhere is the skill of the Incas better shown than in their buildings. By 1500, the empire contained an enormous number of stone buildings, even in cities like Machu Picchu, high up in the mountains. These were created by countless hours of back-breaking work.

Inca workers quarried the stone by hand in the same manner as the ancient Egyptians. They enlarged natural faults in the rockface, inserting wet wooden wedges which swelled to crack the rock. The blocks which split off the rockface were dragged to the building site using rollers, levers, sledges and ropes. When high walls or terraces were being built, the Incas made earth ramps up which the massive stone blocks could be pulled. These were then levered into place.

SHAPING STONE

The builders shaped the blocks with stone axes and obsidian pebbles, and smoothed the edges with sand. Using these simple tools, the Incas produced impressive stonework with joints so tight that not even the thinnest knife could be driven in. The stones were not regular in shape and no two were quite the same size. They had many faces and some had as many as 30 corners. Yet in every Inca building all the stones interlock precisely. Each stone, even those weighing many tonnes, must have been tried in place time after time to test the fit. This alone shows the amazing persistence and skill of the Inca builders.

Remains of buildings in the Inca city of Pisac. The ruins in the foreground were once a sacred ceremonial centre. The Incas learned their craft from cultures which had developed stoneworking before they did.

In some areas, the Incas made adobe (mud bricks) using wooden moulds. This was a much quicker way of building houses, though the results were less permanent.

FOOD AND FARMING

Inca farms were usually situated midway between the valleys and highland pastures. The peasant farmers could therefore grow more than one food crop and also raise animals. This helped them vary their diet and avoid starvation if a whole crop was lost. Any surplus foods were stored in *qollas*, ready for distribution by officials when food became scarce.

STAPLE FOODS

What the Incas ate depended on the area where they lived. However, all Incas depended on certain staple (basic) foods. In mountainous regions, the staple food was the potato. When the potatoes had been harvested, they were left outside at night to freeze. Then they were dried in the hot sun. This process of freeze-drying produced *chuñu*, a food that could be stored for long periods. At lower altitudes, the Incas grew maize, which also could be kept for long periods and eaten when other foods were scarce.

Inca farmers used the taclla *or foot-plough to dig the ground. The men stood in lines moving backwards as they dug up the earth with their ploughs. The women crouched in front of the men, breaking up the earth with hoes called* lampas, *and planting.*

The Incas used reed boats, similar to these, when fishing on inland waters. Boats like this are still used today. The Incas used rafts made from balsa wood to make sea journeys.

THE FARMING YEAR

There were two main seasons in the farming year: the wet season (lasting from October to May), and the dry season (from June to September). The times for planting, harvesting and tilling the soil followed a strict pattern. August, the month for ploughing, always began with a festival in which the nobles played an important role:

'If the Sapa Inca himself or his governor or some high official happened to be present, he started the work with a golden digging stick which they brought to the Inca, and following his example all the other officials and nobles who accompanied him did the same.'

Padre Coba

A VARIED DIET

Many of the foods which we enjoy now, such as avocados, peppers, tomatoes and chocolate, were first produced by Andean farmers. Coca and a rice-like grain called *quinoa* were grown in some parts of the empire. In tropical areas, the Incas grew guavas and cactus. People who lived near the coasts caught and dried fish. Wildfowl, such as duck, were also eaten and most people kept a few guinea pigs for meat.

MEALS

Most Incas began their day with a snack at dawn. They drank *a'ka*, a thick, mildly alcoholic, malty drink and ate what was left of the previous evening's supper. They ate a substantial meal at midday. The Incas did not know how to fry, and boiled most of their food. A favourite dish was *mote* which was maize cooked with peppers and herbs. Sun-dried llama meat and powdered *chuñu* was made into a stew called *locro*. They baked a kind of bread made from ground maize and cooked in the ashes of the fire. They knew how to make popcorn and thought it a delicacy.

FORMAL MEALS

Supper was eaten between four and five o'clock. The food was placed in cooking pots on a cloth on the ground. The men squatted around and helped themselves. They ate with their fingers although they would drink soup from bowls. The women, who had done all the cooking, sat outside the circle with their backs to the men. An important guest, such as a *curaca*, sat in the place of honour.

An Inca pot made of clay which was used to carry water. The long narrow neck makes it harder to spill the water and easier to pour it out.

WOMEN

Women played a vital role in Inca society. They acted as wives, mothers, servants, farm-workers and servants of the Sun God. But like all Incas they had little choice about what they did. It was the Inca state which decided which careers they would follow. Once they had been set on their chosen paths, there was little opportunity to turn back.

An Inca marriage ceremony. The couples married by a simple ceremony of holding hands and exchanging sandals.

THE LEFT-OUT GIRLS

When they had reached 10 years of age, all Inca girls were put into one of two groups at the annual census. The visiting *runaquipa* sent the most beautiful young girls away to be trained as Chosen Women. The larger group, known as the 'left-out' girls, remained in their villages. Here they learned all the domestic skills they would need in life, particularly spinning, weaving and cooking.

MARRIAGE

When they became 12 years old, the 'left-out' girls were old enough to marry. Every year, the *curaca* held a marriage market where husbands were chosen for them. All boys who had reached the age of 24 had to attend the market. The couples married by a simple ceremony of holding hands and exchanging sandals. The women spent the rest of their lives classed as 'warriors' wives', raising their families and helping with the farming.

THE CHOSEN WOMEN

The other group of physically perfect girls were known as *acclacunas* (Chosen Women). There were as many as 15,000 Chosen Women in Peru at any one time. The girls were trained as Chosen Women in *Mamacona* institutes. These institutes were rather like convents and situated close to large towns. The largest, near Cuzco, contained almost 1,500 women.

LEARNING DUTIES

The girls were supervised by older, unmarried Chosen Women called *mamacuans*, who were regarded as wives of the Sun God. The girls learnt about the rituals surrounding the Sun religion. They also learnt how to cook and to weave vicuña wool into the best quality cloth called *kumbi*. The *mamacuans* made clothes from the *kumbi*, which could only be worn by the Sapa Inca and his chief wife (who was known as the *coya*).

PRIESTESSES OF THE SUN

Their training over, the girls were divided again. Many became priestesses called the Handmaidens of the Sun. They were sent to temples of the Sun where they assisted in the worship of all the Inca's gods, although they mainly served the Sun God. They prepared ceremonial food and drink, especially a maize beer called *chicha* which was drunk in large amounts during festivals. A few Chosen Women were singled out to be sacrificed, perhaps the greatest honour of all.

Domestic chores like cooking and spinning were done by women. Here a young woman is grinding corn cobs into flour using a heavy stone handmill. Behind her, another woman is spinning wool that has been washed and combed.

NOBLE WIVES

Some of the Chosen Women became the wives or concubines of high officials or famous generals, members of the royal *ayllu*. Some were sent to the House of the Inca's Chosen Women. Here they became the wives of the Sapa Inca himself. Most Sapa Incas had hundreds of wives. Atahuallpa was reported to have had 700.

As a result, each Sapa Inca had many descendants from whom he could chose his court, his chief administrators and his successor. All of the Inca's sons were considered to be of equal rank and the eldest son did not necessarily become the next Sapa Inca. This led to many plots and revolts in the royal family, particularly at the start of a new reign, as each son might try to gain power.

Handmaidens of the Sun tended the sacred fire inside the Sun temples. There were sun temples throughout the empire. The handmaidens lived protected lives like nuns, watched over by senior priestesses.

The coya was the most important of all the Sapa Inca's wives. She was waited on hand and foot by the daughters of nobles. This illustration of a Sapa Inca's coya was drawn by Poma de Ayala in 1620.

KEEPING POWER

The most important woman in the Inca empire was the Sapa Inca's sister. This was because the Sapa Inca married his own sister, taking her as his chief wife, the *coya*, which means 'star'. She was the only legitimate wife of the Sapa Inca, and she lived a life of great luxury. Only the Sapa Inca was allowed to marry his sister. In this way he made sure that his divinity was passed on to his descendants.

23

HOMES

O rdinary Incas spent most of their lives outside, working. What little spare time they had was occupied by eating and sleeping. Therefore most of their homes were simple shelters designed to protect them from the worst effects of the cold, rain and snow. As good farming land was so scarce in Peru, houses were usually built on rocky or barren land where crops could not be grown.

HOUSES

Most Incas lived in rectangular houses built of adobe bricks or rocks plastered with mud. The roof was held up with wooden poles. Most houses had just a single window and one door that were simple openings in the wall covered with woollen curtains. The roof was thickly thatched with grass. Inside, the floor was of beaten earth. On this was a simple hearth made from stones arranged in a rough circle. There was no chimney, and the smoke from the cooking fire drifted out through the thatched roof.

FURNITURE

The houses had no proper furniture. People sat or slept on llama skins, woollen blankets or reed mats. Some houses had stone benches built into the walls and niches which held small statues of Inca gods. Incas used pegs to hang up their possessions. Ordinary peasants did not own very much, but they might each have had an extra tunic, a shawl, a decorated cloak for wearing at festivals and a sling. If the husband was a warrior, he would hang up his warrior's fighting tunic, his helmet, and his shield which would be decorated with his *aylłu's* totem (badge).

CITY HOUSES

There were some differences between city and village houses. These were largely due to the way city houses were adapted to fit into the available space. Machu Picchu, situated high up in the Andes, is the best preserved example of an Inca city. The see-through scene here shows how city houses were not all the same size or shape. There were some larger houses and some with two storeys. The upper floors of houses were probably reached by a ladder. This may have been made of rope rather than of wood, given the lack of trees at this altitude. Some houses had a lengthwise stone wall that divided them into two completely separate homes.

WONDERFUL STONEWORK

Rocky features were built into some houses. In one house at Machu Picchu, for example, a large rock was carved into a quern for grinding grain. The walls of many houses were built of shaped stone blocks fitted together without mortar (see pages 18-19). This produced buildings well able to withstand earthquakes.

1 Two-storey house
2 Door into upper storey from higher terrace
3 Possessions hanging on pegs
4 Two-storey building divided into two homes.
5 Roof tied onto pegs in walls
6 Single-storey house
7 Hollowed rock used for grinding grain or storing water
8 Open-fronted building used for storage or as a workshop

An Inca featherwork fan. Many of the brightly coloured feathers the Incas used to make their intricate feather mosaics and other types of featherwork came from birds caught in the Amazon jungle.

This pottery figure shows an Inca porter carrying a bottle-shaped pot called an aryballos. *The pot would balance perfectly on its pointed bottom when full.*

Almost everyone in Inca society did some kind of craft work. Like all activities within the Inca Empire, the work was highly organized. Though some craftwork was done at home, much of it was done by groups of workers in large workshops like factories.

TEXTILES

Cloth-making was probably the most important craft activity. Cotton was grown in the lowlands, but wool was the main Andean material. Alpaca wool, easy to work because of its fine quality, was used to make *awaka*, the most widely used type of cloth. *Awaka* was usually white, mixed with greys and natural browns. Llama wool, which was coarse and greasy, was spun as fibre for blankets, sacks, ropes and llama halters. The best quality cloth came from vicuña wool, which was soft and silky.

MAKING THE CLOTH

After the animals had been sheared, the wool was divided out among members of the *ayllu*. Any surplus was stored in official storage bins at the *qollas*. Although Incas often used raw wool, they were skilled in the art of dyeing. They dyed much of the wool before spinning it. They also knew how to tie-dye the finished cloth, producing a patchwork of brilliant colours. Dyes came from plants and from dried cochineal insects which gave a vivid red.

The thread was spun on drop spindles fitted with ceramic whorls. Weaving was done by both men and women, although women worked with the finest wools. Most cloth was produced on a backstrap or belt loom. One end of the cloth was tied round a tree or other upright object and the other end was tied as a belt around the weaver's back. The weavers kept the cloth taut by leaning backwards as they wove.

Most Inca garments were made by joining rectangular pieces of cloth together, as in this poncho. The hole for the head was simply a slit or slits where the material was not joined. The Incas made little attempt to cut their garments to fit the shape of the body.

FANCY CLOTH

Some skilled workers made tunics from the brilliantly-coloured feathers of jungle birds. They also made cloth called *cahquira* which was decorated with bangles of gold or tiny bells and golden specks. Some tunics were completely covered with gold, silver or burnished copper pieces. Tunics such as these were probably worn by the nobility at feasts or religious festivals.

POTTERY

The Incas were skilful potters. They were able to make their pottery, some of which was very fine, without using a potter's wheel. The Inca potter rolled the clay into sausage shapes and coiled them to make a pot. The sides of the pot were smoothed with a small wooden tool shaped like a flat disk. The pots were dried in the sun, painted with geometric or animal designs, and then fired to harden them.

Inca pottery was both practical and decorative. Potters made three-legged pots which were used by soldiers on campaign and large, elegant pots, rather like Grecian urns. Another popular design was the whistling pot. When the pot was emptied, air was drawn in, making a whistling sound. These pots often showed a person playing a flute or a whistle.

THE SWEAT OF THE SUN

The Incas produced huge quantities of gold and silver, which they called 'sweat of the Sun' and 'tears of the Moon'. Most of the gold was found in rivers, by washing it out of river gravel (panning). The Incas also mined for gold and silver in the mountains. It has been estimated that as much as 200,000 kilograms of gold was produced annually. Many Incas paid their labour tax by working in the mines, digging for precious metals.

THE SAPA INCA'S GOLD

Each grain of metal mined or panned was recorded on *quipus*. Precious metals belonged to the Sapa Inca and had to be sent to Cuzco. Here goldsmiths used many different methods to work the metal. They made a huge number of gold objects. Important buildings were often sheathed in gold panels. After the death of a Sapa Inca, a life-size gold statue was made of him. His palace, which became his tomb, was ornamented in gold. The Spanish reported seeing gardens filled with plants, trees and animals all made of gold. Sadly, few of these wonderful golden objects have survived as the Spanish conquerors melted most of them down.

This silver figurine of a woman chewing coca leaves is a fine example of the skill of Inca silversmiths.

Women weaving llama wool on belt looms. These portable looms were used in many parts of Central and South America.

CLOTHES AND FASHIONS

Noble Incas wore golden ear plugs. These ones show a warrior carrying a spear and shield, picked out in semi-precious stones.

The clothes worn by the Incas, from the most powerful noble to the humblest worker, were very similar in style. Nevertheless, there were many variations in the colours, patterns and quality of the garments. However, where people lived had more effect on what they wore. In the high mountains, for example, the Incas wore many layers of clothes made principally from alpaca wool. In the warmer lowlands, light clothes made from cotton were more practical.

This rich Inca family is preparing to attend a festival. Though the clothes worn by the Incas were similar in style and shape, only noble Incas would have worn clothes as fine as these.

MEN'S CLOTHES

All Inca men wore the breechclout, which was a length of cloth worn around the waist. It was made of cotton or wool and held in place by a colourful belt made of woven wool. Over this many Inca men wore a tunic called an *onka*. This was a simple garment, usually made of alpaca wool, which looked a bit like a poncho. During cold weather or in higher areas an Inca wrapped himself in a *yacolla*, or cape, which was also made of wool. He wore sandals on his feet and braided his hair with coloured woollen strings. During festivals, men wore highly decorated tunics which reached down to their ankles.

WOMEN'S CLOTHES

All Inca women dressed in the *anacu*. This was an ankle-length tunic, woven from alpaca wool. It was held in place with a sash. Over this the woman wore a shawl called a *topo* which she fastened with a copper, silver or gold pin, depending on her rank in society. Women also braided, bound and tied their hair with woollen ribbons. Like the men, they wore sandals on their feet.

Inca onkas *or ponchos. The cantuta flowers on the white poncho were popular in Inca times and are now the state emblem of Peru. The base of the poncho on the left is woven cloth into which the quills of hundreds of feathers have been pushed. The design, which shows birds, is created by using feathers of different colours. A cloak as magnificent as this would have been worn by someone very important.*

NOBLES' CLOTHING

Although Inca nobles dressed in a similar style to the ordinary workers, their garments were of much better quality. Their ponchos and breechclouts were woven from the finest vicuña wool. On special occasions they wore more exotic garments, such as mantles made from dyed birds' feathers. The Sapa Inca, Atahuallpa, was described by one of the Spanish conquistadors (conquerors) as wearing a dark mantle made of bat skins.

SYMBOLS OF AUTHORITY

Eminent Incas wore or carried special objects as symbols of their authority. The Sapa Inca carried a golden-headed mace, which was decorated with a stiffened pennant. He wore a fringe of red tassels lined with gold lamé (fabric woven with gold and silver thread). An official called a *totrioc michoc*, whose job it was to rule the provinces and act as judge, had ear lobes which were split open to hang down the sides of his cheeks. Feather headdresses and gold jewellery marked out other important officials, such as priests.

PIERCED EARS

Noble Incas could often be distinguished by the massive ear plugs they wore. The plugs were usually made of gold. Noble men pierced their ears at an early age and wore rounded golden and jewelled disks in the holes. Gradually the size of these ear plugs was increased. This stretched the holes until they became large enough to pass an egg through.

Ear plugs showed the status of their wearer. The larger and more splendid the ear plugs, the more powerful and important the wearer. For example, the most powerful priests were known as *orejons*, which meant 'big ears', after their huge ear plugs. The Sapa Inca had the most splendid and enormous ear plugs of all.

This rectangular bag was made of woven wool and decorated with small gold plates. It was worn slung over the shoulder.

29

GROWING UP

An 11th-13th century Chancay woollen doll made from woven cloth. Inca children would have played with dolls similar to this.

An Inca mother places her baby in its elaborate wooden cradle. The baby was strapped tightly in. The cradle could be left on the ground or slung on the mother's back so the baby was carried in a vertical position looking backwards.

Children were trained from birth for their future role in the community. For most this meant learning to suffer cold and hunger without complaint, and to obey without question the orders given to them by their superiors.

A COLD START

There were no Inca midwives. A mother gave birth, gave her baby a quick wash in the nearest stream and then returned to work. This harsh beginning set the pattern for Inca childhood. Soon after birth, a baby received a ritual hair-cutting called *rutu-chicoy* and was given a temporary name. For the first two years of its life, however, a child was likely to be called simply *wawa* or baby. On the fourth day after birth the baby was placed in a cradle or *quirau*.

A STERN CHILDHOOD

From birth, babies were washed in cold water every morning, then wrapped tightly in cloth. The cold dip was believed to strengthen the child's legs and arms and help it withstand the severe mountain climate. Babies were breastfed until they were two or three years old.

According to Garcilaso de la Vega, babies were fed at regular intervals. He said they were never fed 'on demand', however much they cried, and did not seem to have been cuddled by their mothers. This stern upbringing helped prepare children for the hardship they might experience as adults.

THE FIRST LESSONS

When a baby was taken out of its cradle it was sometimes kept in a deep hole which acted as a kind of playpen. Up to the age of two, children were classified as *saya huamrac* or 'those able to stand'. Although during the first two years of a child's life Inca parents were allowed to look after their children, they did not play with them much. Children were expected to learn to crawl and walk without any help.

In spite of this harsh beginning, babies were always looked after. Even unwanted babies were not simply abandoned by their mothers. The Incas had a number of state orphanages where unwanted babies could be cared for.

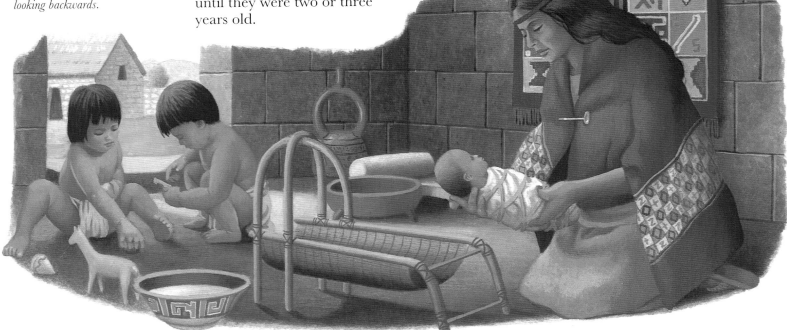

LEARNING USEFUL SKILLS

Once a baby was two years old it was classified as a member of the group of 'bread receivers'. Children were still allowed to play, but they now had to learn useful skills and begin to take on responsibilities. Punishments for children who misbehaved could be very severe. Most of the lessons were learned from older members of the *ayllu*. Peasant children were probably taught the various Inca customs and taboos. The sons of nobles had tutors called *amataus*. They were taught the main rites and beliefs of Sun worship, the chief laws, and given some instruction in politics and military matters.

Having endured tests of his courage, a noble boy swears loyalty to the Sapa Inca and receives his first sling, shield and mace.

BECOMING AN ADULT

At puberty, a boy was given a permanent name. When he was 14 he attended the most important ceremony of his life at which he received his breechclout. This symbolized becoming a man. The sons of nobles went on a pilgrimage to the birth-place of the Inca state in the Cuzco valley. There, each boy had to endure tests of his courage, strength and discipline. He attended various religious ceremonies during which llamas were sacrificed and blood was smeared on his face. He swore an oath of loyalty to the Sapa Inca and received his sling, shield and mace. At the end of the sixth day the boy's ears were pierced, his first ear plugs were inserted and he officially became a warrior in the Sapa Inca's elite guards.

PREPARING FOR MARRIAGE

Young girls came of age and were named at about the same age as boys. This occasion was marked with a hair-combing ceremony. Girls married soon after this. By the time a male descendant of the Sapa Inca was ready to marry, he had received as thorough an education as possible in a land without schools. He had gone with the Sapa Inca on tours of the empire, fought in battles, learned the important rituals of Sun worship and heard the most important stories in Inca history.

This simple pottery model shows a mother holding her baby as she carries a huge pot on her back.

31

TEMPLES OF THE SUN

The Incas had many gods, beliefs and superstitions. As well as worshipping the Sun God and a host of other gods, they believed that everyone had a *hauqui* or guardian spirit. They revered holy objects and places they called *huacas*. Each *ayllu* had its own *huaca*. Pachacuti made Coricancha, the Temple of the Sun in Cuzco, the *huaca* for the whole empire.

GODS

The main god was Viracocha, the god of creation. But the most widely worshipped and powerful god was *Inti*, the Sun God, who gave heat, light, life and fertility. Second to *Inti* in power was the Moon, the Sun's wife. The Earth, the sea, Venus, and constellations representing animals such as llamas and pumas, were also worshipped. *Illapa*, god of thunder and war, controlled hail and rain. The sharp crack of his sling, as he let loose a thunderbolt, was heard as the breaking of a storm.

ORACLES AND SOOTHSAYERS

The Incas were a superstitious people who would not do anything important without first asking a soothsayer to consult the spirits on their behalf. Soothsayers also foretold the future and studied omens to discover who might be guilty of a crime.

If a drought, earthquake or other disaster occurred, soothsayers might recommend making sacrifices of cloth, miniature figures or animals. The sacrifice of white llamas was considered specially effective, although a poor person might satisfy the gods with a guinea pig. In times of dire crisis, the Incas sacrificed humans.

This is a great temple to the Sun God, built by the Incas. In the background are priests' houses and storehouses. When you lift up the see-through page you can see a procession of priests and a sacrificial llama winding its way through the temple. At the top of the page is revealed Coricancha, the magnificent temple in Cuzco.

TEMPLE OF THE SUN GOD
1 Image of Sun God
2 Procession of priests
3 Adobe wall on stone base
4 Niche containing idol
5 Priests' houses
6 Storehouses

CORICANCHA
7 House of the Sun
8 Garden of golden
   maize and llamas

CORICANCHA

The Incas built many temples where they worshipped their gods. Cuzco's Coricancha, where the Sun God was principally worshipped, was a spectacular building. The temple walls were covered with sheets of gold inside and out. They contained six rectangular 'chapels' which opened on to a central courtyard. The chapels, which were dedicated to the Sun, Moon, the Pleiades (a cluster of stars), Thunder, Lightning and the Rainbow, were all decorated with gold or silver. At the eastern end of the courtyard was a huge plate of solid gold which represented the Sun. Under this, seated on golden thrones and dressed in royal robes, sat the embalmed bodies of previous Inca rulers.

PRIESTS AND DOCTORS

A Chimu gold ceremonial knife with a llama on the handle decorated with turquoise. Knives similar to this were used by Inca priests during religious ceremonies - perhaps even for human sacrifice.

Priests ran the temples and organized the religious ceremonies which were such an important part of the Incas' life. There were so many priests that some historians think there were more of them than soldiers in Peru. More than 4,000 people worked at Coricancha alone as priests or Handmaidens of the Sun, or in humbler roles as shepherds of the Sun God's flocks, porters of his goods and sweepers of his floors.

THE HIGH PRIEST

The power and importance of any priest depended on the shrine where he worked and the tasks he did there. Sun priests had more prestige and influence than other priests. The most important priest of all was the *vilcaoma*, the High Priest of the Sun, who was always a close relative of the Sapa Inca. He led a very simple life, but he and the priests who assisted him were all nobles. They formed an inner circle that wielded great power and influence at court. Away from Cuzco, the priests who worked in the temples of the Sun and for the great *huacas* all came from families of the *curacas*. The least important priests were those appointed by each village to serve their local gods.

A young priestess is taken by priests to be sacrificed to the Sun God. Human sacrifice was only carried out by the Incas in times of dire emergency, such as a long drought or a major earthquake.

DOCTORS

Inca priests also acted as doctors. Some of their 'cures' seem more like magic than medicine, and involved charms, trances, chants and spells. Amongst the charms the Incas thought most effective were 'bezoars'. These were stones eaten by some animals, such as the tapir, to aid their digestion.

But in some ways Inca doctors were far in advance of European doctors of the times. Inca doctors could cure many serious illnesses including dysentery, ulcers, eye problems, lice and toothache. They used a wide variety of sensible and effective herbal medicines which they got from *hampi camayoc*, the keepers of authorized remedies or state chemists. They also got medicines from *collahuaya*, or pedlars, who carried medicinal plants, amulets and lucky charms. One of the most effective Inca medicines was quinine which was used to dress wounds and sores, and to cure fever.

An Inca worshipping at a huaca. *The tower in the background is a* chullpa - *a type of burial tower built by the Tiahuanacoans. The Incas learned some of their stoneworking skills from this earlier civilization.*

SURGEON-PRIESTS

Inca priests were also skilled surgeons who could amputate crushed or diseased limbs, and even perform brain operations. Most villages had a *sancoyoc* or surgeon-priest who could treat broken limbs, open abscesses or pull out teeth. The most skilful surgeons travelled with the army or treated nobles in the large cities. The surgeon-priests anaesthetized their patients by making them chew coca leaves, drink large amounts of *chicha*, or by hypnosis. They performed operations using knives made of flint, obsidian, gold, copper or silver. They knew how to burn wounds to prevent infection. They bit off the heads of large ants and used the jaws as clips to close wounds, just as modern surgeons use stitches.

BLOOD TRANSFUSIONS

We know that surgeon-priests performed blood transfusions about 500 years before the practice became common elsewhere in the world. As all the Incas belonged to the same blood group (O rhesus positive), bad reactions in a patient were rare.

DEATH AND BURIAL

When an Inca died, his or her body might be mummified and treated as a sacred object. Graves were treated with great respect as dead people were believed to protect the living. Members of a dead person's family visited their relative's grave regularly to make offerings, perhaps of flowers or food. Failure to make the necessary offerings and sacrifices invited the wrath of the dead person's spirit. The shrines of the dead were tended by old men who were no longer able to do heavy manual work.

An Inca priest performs a magic cure. We now know that the mind can play an important role in illness. Perhaps the treatments performed by Inca doctors were more successful with patients who believed strongly in the power of the Sun God.

An Inca surgeon trepanned, or cut open, this deformed skull, perhaps to let out evil spirits, or perhaps to make the skull into a more regular shape. It would be interesting to know how long the patient survived.

THE ARMY

The sling was the favoured long-range weapon of the Incas. The sling, shown above with a sling stone, is made entirely of wool. Below it are two club heads made of obsidian.

The Inca army was almost always victorious in battle because it was bigger, could usually move faster and was better organized than the tribes against which it fought.

PART-TIME SOLDIERS

The only full-time army in the empire was the Sapa Inca's bodyguard of about 10,000 soldiers. These soldiers were recruited from the nobility. Other soldiers were usually ordinary farmers. Each province had to supply a certain number of able-bodied men for the army. The actual number depended on the size of the province's population.

ARMOUR AND WEAPONS

Soldiers wore quilted cotton protective tunics and wooden or plaited cane helmets with woollen fringes. Their backs were protected by plates of iron-hard chonta wood. Soldiers carried shields made from wood or toughened hide.

At close quarters the Incas usually fought with clubs. These were usually metre-long wooden shafts tipped with heavy bronze or stone heads shaped like a star. The Incas also fought with spears and with two-handed swords made of hard chonta wood.

STOREHOUSES

The Inca army was served by an excellent supply system. Supplies were kept in the thousands of *qollas* scattered throughout the empire. In peacetime they protected the Incas from the worst effects of famine. In wartime they ensured that an army on campaign was as well fed and equipped as an army resting in Cuzco. Some *qollas* were stocked with a huge variety of food including *chuño*, dried meat and *cumo* (various conserved foods which could be eaten without cooking). Other storehouses were full of cloaks, wool, cloth and military equipment. Some supplies were carried with the army on llamas. The llamas could also be slaughtered for food.

GOING TO WAR

When war broke out, the *qollas* were filled with supplies. Great numbers of warriors were summoned and put into companies according to their *ayllus*. The army set out along the excellent roads.

In the meantime, ambassadors were sent to the trouble spot. There they made terrible threats, but also promised gifts and honour if the enemy surrendered. If the enemy refused, the Inca army attacked with great violence. There were few battle tactics. The slingers tossed their stones and then the warriors closed in with maces. The battle soon became a chaotic mêlée which the Incas nearly always won by sheer force of numbers.

The Incas used a few simple tactics such as setting fire to the grass to confuse their enemies, and dividing their forces and attacking from two sides. But once the two armies joined battle they just fought fiercely until one side won.

TERRIBLE REVENGE

Defeated enemies were slaughtered and their heads were cut off. Skulls were plated with gold and made into goblets. Enemy teeth were made into necklaces. Captives were paraded through Cuzco and laid in front of the Sun temple while the Sapa Inca trod on their necks as a symbol of victory. Some prisoners were flayed and their skins made into bizarre drums in the shape of the human body. When the drum was played the dead soldier appeared to be beating his own belly with drumsticks.

THE INCAS TAKE CONTROL

After conquest a census was taken. Local gods, customs, dress and language were respected but the defeated tribe had to agree to worship the Sun God. Local chieftains were either put to death or sent to Cuzco to learn *Quechua* and be trained in Inca ways. A clay relief model of the conquered area, along with the census of people, animals and produce, was taken to Cuzco. A*yllus* were established along Inca lines. Roads were extended into the conquered area. Architects were sent to build new towns and a temple to the Sun God. If the population was hostile it was removed to another area and loyal people called *mitimaes* were moved in to replace them. The area became an Inca province.

Golden skull cups were made from the skulls of the Incas' fiercest enemies. They were carried by the generals as ceremonial objects.

An Inca general is carried to battle on a litter as he whirls his sling round his head. This picture was drawn in about 1620, long after the Spanish conquest, so it may not be entirely accurate.

37

There was no form of wheeled transport in the Inca empire, because the Incas had not invented the wheel. Neither did they have horses, so most people had to go by foot. They travelled on the spectacular roads which stretched **23,000** kilometres through the Inca lands. This amazing road system was one of the major reasons for the success of the Inca empire.

Inca suspension bridges were made of braided ropes called cabuya *which were plaited and twisted into cables as thick as a human's body. Several cables spanned the river and were anchored by massive stone pillars and heavy stone weights. Wood and bamboo planks laid across the cables formed the floor of the bridge.*

THE IMPORTANCE OF ROADS

Inca roads were the veins and arteries of the empire. Along them marched the Inca armies as they moved to repel invading Amazonian tribes or conquer new lands. The roads were important supply routes for llama trains carrying goods from one part of the empire to another. They were also a vital communication network along which travelled the messengers and officials who were the eyes, ears and voice of the Sapa Inca.

FEATS OF ENGINEERING

Many Inca roads crossed high mountains. On steep slopes Inca engineers built stone steps which looked like giant flights of stairs. These steps were no obstacle to travellers on foot or to the sure-footed llamas and guanacos used as pack animals. The Incas also built special jungle roads, wide military roads, gold roads and royal roads. The Andean royal road, which was 5,200 kilometres long, was longer than the longest Roman road. Inca engineers developed special techniques to deal with particular problems. They built low walls alongside roads in desert areas to stop sand drifting over the road's surface. In swamps they raised roads on stone causeways.

BRIDGES

Where roads had to cross steep valleys or ravines, Inca engineers built bridges. They used reed boats as pontoons to bridge wide, slow-flowing rivers. These were common around Lake Titicaca where reeds were plentiful. The Incas also built simple cantilever bridges to cross narrow streams. However, their most spectacular bridges were suspension bridges built across deep ravines.

THE BEAUTIFUL ROAD

The main Inca highway was known as *Capac-nan*, 'the Beautiful Road'. It ran from Cuzco to Quito and was over 2,400 kilometres long. Built from dovetailed blocks of stone, the road was arrow-straight for most of its length and a uniform 8 metres wide. In common with many Inca roads, trees were planted alongside the Beautiful Road to give travellers shade. A canal shadowed the course of the road, carrying a stream of fresh water so travellers could quench their thirst and water their beasts. Every 25-40 kilometres there were *tampus* (rest houses) where messengers and travellers could stay the night (see pages 40-41).

MARKETS

Many of the people travelling on the Inca roads were traders. However, trade was very limited. Only those goods not set aside for the Sapa Inca or the Sun God could be traded. There was little trade with people outside the empire.

Trade took place at local markets called *catus*. The Incas had no money so they used a system known as *trueque* for exchanging goods. People from the highlands swapped llama wool, *chuñu* and *charki* (dried meat) for lowland products such as salt, fish, maize, cotton, fruits and beans. Jungle people brought feathers, iron-hard palm chonta wood, birds, dyes, rubber, tobacco and drugs. Everyone traded for manufactured goods such as cloth, pottery and carvings. Exchange was busiest in the harvest season.

Teams of workers did labour duty building and repairing the Beautiful Road. The road passed through steamy swamps, teeming rainforest, icy plateaus and arid desert. It spanned huge ravines by means of suspension bridges. In places it rose to over 5,000 metres.

MESSENGERS

The Sapa Inca kept in touch with all the corners of the empire through a network of messengers. Messages were learnt by heart or recorded on *quipus*.

MESSENGERS

Inca messengers were known as *chasquis*. They were chosen from the fittest and fastest young men. Groups of between four and six *chasquis* lived in cabins built at intervals beside the main roads. Two of them would always be acting as lookouts.

RELAYING A MESSAGE

As soon as a messenger, easily recognizable because of the large white feathered headdress he wore, was spotted in the distance, one of the *chasquis* would race to meet him. The *chasquis* ran beside the incoming messenger, listening while the message was repeated to him. If the messenger carried a *quipu*, the *chasquis* would take it from him.

Once he was sure he had the message perfectly by heart, the *chasquis* ran on towards the next relay station leaving the tired messenger to rest in the cabin. In this way messages could travel over 240 kilometres in a single day.

EMERGENCY MESSAGES

If a message brought news of an emergency, such as an invasion or a rebellion, a signal could be sent by a chain of bonfires. As each group of *chasquis* saw smoke or flames rising from the next relay station, they lit a bonfire of their own. In this way news of the peril flashed to Cuzco more speedily than the fastest runner. The Sapa Inca could order his army to set out at once, marching towards the bonfires before the actual cause of the alarm was known. The general marching with the soldiers knew he would eventually meet one of the messengers on the route and learn from him the exact nature of the emergency.

1 **Hall where travellers, messengers and soldiers could stay**
2 **Soldiers erecting a tent**
3 **Small temple**
4 **Royal or official's apartment**
5 **Sunken bath**
6 **Signal fire**
7 **Llama pen**

INCA WAYSTATIONS

The Incas built waystations called *tampus* at intervals along the roads. Some of these were probably little more than simple cabins where tired messengers could rest. Others seem to have been much more elaborate centres.

On the larger sites, archeological excavations have revealed remains of what were probably halls used for official and military business and where travellers could stay, royal apartments where the Sapa Inca and his family would rest, and a temple where travellers could worship the Sun God. The remains of storehouses and baths have also been found.

The see-through scene below shows a waystation, with a unit of the Inca army arriving. A few of the soldiers will be able to stay in the long hall on the right. The rest of the patrol will have to sleep in the open; we know the Inca soldiers used tents. When the see-through page is turned, you can see inside the hall as well as the apartments and offices in the compound on the left. A soldier is pointing at smoke rising from behind the hills - is this a warning of an enemy army?

41

Francisco Pizarro, the conqueror of Peru. He was about 57 years old in 1532 and could neither read nor write. He was drawn to Tumbes by hints and rumours that a rich empire lay somewhere to the south. After his soldiers had destroyed the Inca empire, he was savagely criticized.

In 1532 a small Spanish ship sailed into the Inca port of Tumbes. It carried 110 foot soldiers, 67 cavalry and one small cannon. This tiny force was led by adventurer Francisco Pizarro. He had been appointed by the King of Spain to be the new governor of Peru. South America was a continent which the Spanish had only just discovered. They knew nothing about the Incas. Pizarro wanted gold and power and he planned to get them by any means. Within a few weeks Pizarro's small body of men had brought the mighty Inca empire to its knees.

DIVISION OF THE EMPIRE

In 1493, when Huayna Capac became Sapa Inca, the empire had reached its greatest power. In 1527, Huayna became very ill, probably from smallpox, a terrible disease brought by Europeans to the New World. The Incas had no immunity against European diseases. It is estimated that as many as 250,000 Incas may have died of smallpox before any of them even saw a European. Huayna died without naming his successor. Many people thought Huáscar, son of Huayna and his *coya*, should be the new Sapa Inca. Others, including many Inca generals, preferred Huayna's elder son, Atahuallpa, whose mother was not the *coya*.

CIVIL WAR

Atahuallpa decided to challenge his brother for the throne. This decision led to a bitter civil war which Atahuallpa finally won. During the ferocious war, thousands of Incas were reported slaughtered in the most appalling atrocities. It was rumoured that Atahuallpa ordered the slaughter of his brother's entire *ayllu*. Over 200 of Huayna's sons were massacred; some were hung, others were weighted with stones and thrown into rivers or lakes, or hurled off cliffs. All Huáscar's female relatives were hung in trees, some by their hair, some by their arms. There was talk that 1,000 enemy warriors had their hearts torn out and scattered on the fields.

How many of these deaths actually happened is hard to say. The Spanish who reported them became the enemies of Atahuallpa, and they might have wanted to exaggerate his crimes to excuse their own terrible deeds.

Pizarro's force landed safely then advanced rapidly inland. Pizarro wanted to impress the Incas with his power. He won several battles and burned those chiefs who opposed him. In this way he quickly subdued the northern part of the empire.

EVENTS AT CAJAMARCA

In November 1532, after winning a great victory and capturing his brother, the triumphant Atahuallpa went to a town called Cajamarca. There, in a camp outside the town, surrounded by 50,000 soldiers fresh from their victory against the forces of Huáscar, Atahuallpa rested and bathed in the hot springs.

Atahuallpa was intrigued to hear that the Spanish strangers were not far away. Atahuallpa was curious about these strangers, but not in the least afraid of them. Meanwhile, Pizarro had moved his small force into the town. He sent a message to Atahuallpa requesting to meet him the next day. The Sapa Inca, carried on his golden litter, arrived with 6,000 unarmed attendants.

AMBUSH

Atahuallpa did not realize that Pizarro had prepared an ambush. The Spanish soldiers hid and waited until the Sapa Inca arrived at the main square. A Spanish priest travelling with Pizarro began to preach to Atahuallpa. The Sapa Inca took the priest's Bible and examined it. Never having seen a book before, Atahuallpa threw it to the ground in disgust. Almost at once, Pizarro gave the signal to attack. The cannon roared, the arquebusiers (musketeers) opened fire and the cavalry charged the Sapa Inca's litter. The Spaniards cut the royal bodyguard down with steel weapons as they tried to defend their lord with their bare hands. Legend says that Pizarro himself seized Atahuallpa and took him prisoner.

Atahuallpa's bodyguard were probably unarmed. They were not expecting an ambush. They were cut down before they could organize any resistance. Once Atahuallpa was a prisoner, the Incas allowed the Spaniards to loot their camp and did not try to rescue their emperor.

Poma de Ayala's 17th century drawing depicts Atahuallpa being shown the Bible by a priest who had travelled with Pizarro's force.

CONQUEST OF THE EMPIRE

By a strange twist of fate, Pizarro had arrived at a time when the Inca empire was divided and weak. By seizing the Sapa Inca, Pizarro cut off the head of power. The Incas, used to obeying orders, did not know what to do and so they did nothing.

A ROOM FULL OF GOLD

Atahuallpa realized that the Spaniards desired gold above everything else. He offered to fill a large room with gold if they would set him free. Pizarro asked that a smaller room nearby should also be filled twice over with silver. Atahuallpa ordered Coricancha to be stripped. The treasure arrived in 200 loads. In one load alone there were 700 plates taken from the walls of the temple. Each of these weighed two kilograms. This single consignment was worth millions of pounds at today's values.

After the defeat of the empire, many Incas became slaves working on coca plantations or in mines, such as the huge workings at Potosi where the Spanish found a whole mountain made of silver ore.

An item of booty seized by the conquistadors. This model of an alpaca is made of silver. Many other fine examples of Inca workmanship were stolen and melted down by the Spaniards.

A FANTASTIC TREASURE

After five months, even though the room had not been filled, Pizarro decided to divide the gold. The first load was intended for the King of Spain. It consisted of some of the finest examples of Inca craftwork. There were goblets, plates, ornaments and vases from temples and royal palaces, and imitations of animals and plants, including golden ears of maize with silver leaves. There was so much treasure that some Spaniards replaced their worn out horse-shoes with silver ones! This first shipment of treasure disappeared on its way to Spain, and was never seen again.

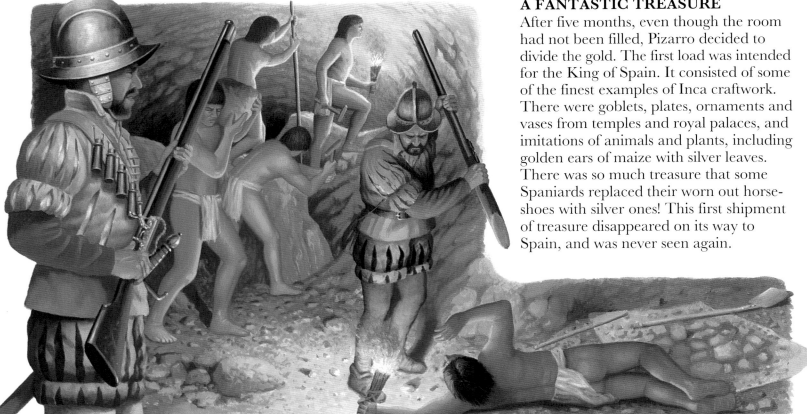

DIVIDING THE TREASURE

The rest of the treasure was shared out among Pizarro's band. Each soldier took more than his own weight in gold and silver. Pizarro took many times that, including the Sapa Inca's throne which was made of solid gold. Pizarro's men, increasingly fearing an Inca attack, began to sleep in full armour. Few of the soldiers would live to spend their wealth.

DEATH OF THE INCA

Now that he had his gold, Pizarro decided to do away with Atahuallpa. He set up a court of the Inquisition (a court where religious 'crimes' were tried). Atahuallpa was accused of murdering his brother Huáscar, of having many wives and of worshipping idols. Atahuallpa was found guilty and sentenced to be burned to death. Appalled because destruction of his body would mean he could not live after his death, Atahuallpa agreed to become a Christian in return for being garrotted (strangled). In spite of the protests of some of Pizarro's followers, the sentence was carried out.

A figurine of a Mamacuan. *She is wearing a piece of cloth with typical Inca patterns on it, coloured with vegetable and mineral dyes. Items like these were often put into tombs, and so a few survived the Spanish conquest.*

Pizarro's actions were criticized by many people in Europe. This cartoon shows him greedily considering the profits of his silver mines.

AFTERMATH

Pizarro then led his soldiers to Cuzco. With no thought to how the Incas would feed themselves, the Spaniards stripped the *qollas* bare. They treated the Incas cruelly and put a puppet Sapa Inca on the throne. Their greed knew no bounds. Inca resistance increased and armed attacks began. Then the Spanish fell out amongst themselves, quarrelling about who should rule what. Eventually some discontented Spaniards plotted against Pizarro and assassinated him on 26 June 1541.

SPANISH RULE

Over the next few years, the Spanish tried to stamp out the old Inca ways. Sun temples were torn down and replaced with Christian churches. Christian missionaries arrived from Spain to convert the Incas to Christianity. Defeated in battle and ravaged by European diseases, the Incas bowed to the inevitable and came forward to be baptized. Many Incas became slave labourers working in the fields and gold mines of their new rulers. Gradually, many aspects of the Inca culture disappeared. In spite of this, some of the old Inca gods and traditions have survived and are now part of a new and vibrant Peruvian culture.

This 16th century Inca beaker is made of wood and decorated with painted scenes showing Spaniards. It may, therefore, have been made shortly after the Spanish invasion.

KEY DATES AND GLOSSARY

We know relatively little about the early history of the Incas. The Incas did not keep written records as we know them, and most of their *quipus* have been destroyed. For this reason the dates given before 1438 can only be approximate.

c3000 BC The coast of Peru is occupied by villagers who live by growing crops and fishing.
c1200 BC Pottery appears.
c800 BC Maize introduced.
c1200 AD Start of Inca civilization, and the reigns of the semi-legendary Incas: Manco Capac, Sinchi Roca, Lloque Yupanqui, Mayta Capac, Capac Yupanqui, Inca Roca, Yahuar Huaca, Viracocha Inca, Pachacuti Inca Yupanqui (1438-1471), Topa Inca Yupanqui (1471-1493) and Huayna Capac (1493-1527).
1527 Pizarro lands at Tumbes and discovers the Inca empire. Civil war between Inca Huascar and his half-brother Atahuallpa (1528-1532).
1532 Pizarro attacks Atahuallpa at Cajamarca. Atahuallpa is taken prisoner and held to ransom for a room full of gold.
1533 Atahuallpa is executed.

1535 Incas conquered by Spaniards. Manco II made Sapa Inca by the Spaniards. Pizarro founds city of Lima.
1537 Manco II escapes to Vilcapampa. He leads an attack on Cuzco but fails to capture the city. When Manco II is killed by Spanish allies, Sayri Tapac, his son, becomes the new Sapa Inca.
1538 Pizarro executes his partner Diego de Almagro after bitter quarrels.
1541 Pizarro killed by followers of Almagro's son.
1560 Sayri Tapac dies of poison. His brother Titu Cusi proclaims himself Sapa Inca and begins a guerilla war against the Spaniards. He dies of a mysterious disease.
1572 Titu Cusi's brother Tupac Amaru becomes Sapa Inca. He is captured by the Spaniards and executed. This marks the end of the Inca empire.
1580 In the 50 years after the conquest, about 6,000,000 former Inca subjects die, mostly of diseases like smallpox brought from Europe by the Spanish invaders.
1780 A *mestizo* (person of mixed Inca and Spanish blood) calling himself Tupac Amaru after one of the last Inca leaders raises an unsuccessful revolt of Indians and *mestizos* against Spanish rule. He is executed in 1781.

The city of Machu Picchu (below) was built high in the mountains about 80 kilometres to the northwest of Cuzco. The Spaniards never found the city, whose ruins were discovered in 1911 by an expedition led by Hiram Bingham.

Glossary

a'ka: a mild alcoholic, malty drink.
ayllu: an Inca clan or social group.
caramayoc: a village headman.
catus: Inca markets.
chasquis: Inca messengers.
chicha: maize beer used in religious ceremonies.
coca: a plant the leaves of which contain several powerful drugs including cocaine.
coya: the Inca Queen, who was also the sister of the Sapa Inca.
curacas: nobles who were not Incas by blood.
huacas: holy objects.
Inti: the Sun God.
lampa: an Inca hoe.
locro: an Inca stew made from dried meat and freeze-dried potato.
mit'a: a compulsory duty to serve in the army or to help build public works.
mitimaes: settlers sent to newly conquered regions to replace the rebellious population.
mote: maize cooked with pepper and herbs.
onka: an Inca tunic worn by men.
orejon: an Inca priest.
qolla: a state-controlled storehouse.
quipu: literally a 'knot', the word was used to describe bundles of knotted cords which the Incas used to record quantities.
quipu camayoc: a person whose job it was to remember what the knots on each *quipu* stood for.

quirau: a cradle for a baby.
runaquipa: an official government counter, so named because of the *quipu* he used to record the count.
sancoyoc: a priest who was also a doctor.
Sapa Inca: the emperor of the Incas. Literally the 'Unique Inca'.
saya huamrac: literally someone able to stand. Used to describe a toddler.
sierra: a mountain range.
taclla: an Inca foot-plough.
Tahuantinsuyu: Land of the Four Quarters, ie the Inca empire. Each quarter was one large province ruled by an official called an *apo* who was always a close relative of the Sapa Inca.
tampus (or tambos): waystations, or rest houses, built on Inca roads.
topo: an Inca shawl.
Viracocha: the Inca god of creation.
wawa: the sound of a baby crying which the Incas used as their word for a baby.

Quotations

Most of the quotations come from letters and memoirs written by Spanish friars working in Peru after the fall of the Inca empire. Many of them learned to speak Quechua, the Incas' language. They wrote down what they could of Inca history and customs. The line drawings were done by Poma de Ayala, a man of mixed Inca and Spanish blood, in the early 17th century.

INDEX